David Hesse

Disney's creative contribution to US-American World War 2 propaganda and its effect on the citizens' attitude towards war

GRIN Verlag

Bibliografische Information der Deutschen Nationalbibliothek:

Die Deutsche Bibliothek verzeichnet diese Publikation in der Deutschen National-
bibliografie; detaillierte bibliografische Daten sind im Internet über http://dnb.d-
nb.de/ abrufbar.

Imprint:

Copyright © 2014 GRIN Verlag GmbH
Druck und Bindung: Books on Demand GmbH, Norderstedt Germany
ISBN: 978-3-656-63754-7

This book at GRIN:

http://www.grin.com/en/e-book/271582/disney-s-creative-contribution-to-us-ameri-
can-world-war-2-propaganda-and

David Hesse

Disney's creative contribution to US-American World War 2 propaganda and its effect on the citizens' attitude towards war

Facharbeit im Leistungskurs Englisch
Friedrich-Harkort-Schule Herdecke
Schuljahr: 2013 / 2014

Table of content

1. My fascination for historical Disney cartoons

For many people, certain characters and figures from movies and series watched in the early years of life still occupy a big, dearly-remembered part of their childhood memories. As for me, Donald, Mickey, and Goofy ought to be called friends and heroes of my personal youth- if not even the ones of, at least, two previous generations. Consequently, (although it might sound naïve) I was personally stunned and befuddled when I first learned about Disney's World War 2 propaganda cartoons which were produced between 1942 and 1945 for the US Government. After having watched some of them on YouTube, I felt like they simply contradicted my childhood experiences, even appearing unreal and fake to me. Yet, further research brought to light their authenticity and revealed a huge range of elements essential to the war effort, which were covered by those cartoons.

When I was to decide for a topic to be dealt with in my 'Facharbeit', the decision was clear: Including my interest in the history and pop culture of the United States of America, Disney's World War 2 cartoons offer a great potential to be researched intensively as one can find a lot of background knowledge, regarding the history of the Disney studios and the general historical context. Also, there is a broad mass of cartoons to be analyzed and looked at closely. Questioning the justification for family cartoons to be used as propaganda material, I further have a firm opinion. However, in order not to go beyond the scope, I must, unfortunately, leave out several relevant and interesting aspects to the topic and do not make any claims for completeness.

In the following, I would like to elucidate my approach towards the issue: To begin with, I focus on general, historical facts about the US-American World War 2 propaganda and Disney's contribution to the war effort, giving basic background information, in order to understand and interpret two war-time cartoons which perfectly exemplify the convincing way most propaganda cartoons worked and appealed to the citizens. Being two of the most popular shorts during World War 2 (one of them even honored with an Oscar) and rather focusing on entertainment, instead of war instructions, both *Der Fuehrer's Face* and *Reason and* Emotion are great fun to watch and very suitable for a detailed interpretation. Eventually, I comment on the general justification of those cartoons and sum up my results.

2. US-American World War 2 propaganda

2.1. General definition of the term 'propaganda'

In general, propaganda can be described as the "attempt to shape or manipulate people's beliefs or actions by means of information (true or false), arguments, or symbols".[1] Hereby, "religious, political, cultural, or commercial messages"[2] are often promoted, using a variety of media, such as print, radio, television, or movies. Although a persistent misconception says propaganda is used by totalitarian regimes only, actually, all governments make use of this persuasive tool which –as broadly assumed- does not simply happen honestly, but involves the "concealment [...] of the truth"[3] or, at least, a "cynical disregard"[4] for it.

One can further distinguish between white and black propaganda: Whereas white propaganda attempts to make the own state policies appear glorious and suitable, black propaganda is to misrepresent the government's enemies.[5]

With regard to Disney's shorts, propagandists have always seen a great way to manipulate their target group by movies because of their ability to speak visually, unite a group and appeal to its individual members, and trigger an emotional reaction, which might further lead to action. Common strategies of movie propaganda comprise "simplification, the prejudicial construction of racial difference, repetition, [and] unanimity". [6]

2.2. Common forms of US-American war-time propaganda, (governmental)
propagandists, and their overall messages and goals

Next to Disney's war-time cartoons, a vast amount of media was used for propaganda purposes by officials seated in the US Government during World War 2: Especially, mass media were made use of to appeal to the citizens, such as motion pictures, the radio, newspapers, newsreels, and others. Hereby, US-American propagandists leaned on techniques of the advertising industry, including "repetition, catchy slogans, [and] celebrity endorsements". [7]

The main coordinator of propaganda was the Office of War Information (OWI). Established by President Roosevelt in 1942, it followed a "strategy of truth"[8], confiding in the

---

[1] Wright (Ed.), A Dictionary of World History
[2] Kuhn, Westwell, A Dictonary of Film Studies
[3] Ebd.
[4] Wright (Ed.) A Dictionary of World History
[5] Cf. McLean, McMillan, The Concise Dictionary of Politics
[6] Cf. Kuhn, Westwell, A Dictionary of Film Studies
[7] Brewer, Why America fights: patriotism and war propaganda from the Philippines to Iraq, p. 98
[8] Ebd., p. 88

critical mind of every mature, well-informed citizen, yet, clearly pointing out the right way to go, namely the support of the war effort. Besides, various more (subordinate) propaganda agencies evolved. Also, the governmental Departments, such as State, War, Navy, and Treasury, owned public information offices.

American propagandists' messages and goals centered around two main ideas: The "fight between democracy and dictatorship"[9], endorsing patriotism for the homeland, and, later on, the fruits of a possible victory, were promoted by the media. According to the US Government, those goals could only be reached by internationalism, the cooperation with allies, pursuing common goals and having common enemies. On the one hand, stressing the importance of a commitment to the war effort to preserve America's future, and on the other hand, revealing the means of the oppressive, freedom-denying dictatorships abroad, governmental propagandists often cleverly combined black and white propaganda. In order to gain more support, one also "reassured cultural beliefs"[10], such as the value of family, making the citizens dream of a "restoration of the old social order"[11] and a prosperous life after the war. Certain information campaigns, dealing with "morale, recruiting, conservation, rationing, manpower, and food"[12], further made an appeal to the citizens to deliver their part to the war effort in daily life, for instance, by growing Victory Gardens or by buying war bonds.

My Kansan host grandmother, Gladys Reimer, did experience some war-time propaganda herself. Being in the age of 7 when Pearl Harbor happened in December 1941, a fair amount of posters was hung up in Junior High which related to the Japanese threat and justified the internment camps where American Japanese were taken to, in order to prevent them from cooperating with the aggressors (see Illus. 1. in appendix).

However, Mennonites –as Gladys and her family- were hardly manipulated and impressed by the propaganda machinery as they did not support the war anyways. Whereas others even dropped out of high school to join the military during wartime, Mennonites refused to salute to the flag. Apparently, they disliked the idea that their children were being snatched up by the US Government to do alternative service, instead of staying around to help on the farm. Due to the family's attitude, Gladys and her siblings were bullied by other kids on the playground and the family sawmill was burned up. [13]

---

[9] Ebd., p. 88
[10] Ebd, p. 89
[11] Ebd., p. 89
[12] Ebd., p. 98
[13] Reimer, personal correspondence

3. Disney's contribution to the war effort

3.1. The studios during wartime

Just a day after Pearl Harbor on December 8, 1941, 500 US Army troops marched into the Disney Studios, in order to protect nearby aircraft factories. Hereby, Disney got in contact with the US Government for the first time and excitedly began producing patriotic movies. [14] Whereas the studios in Burbank, California, had only produced entertaining material in the pre-war period (with the exception of some battle films for the Canadian Government in 1939), now, 94 % were created in service of nearly every branch of the US Government- a total of 400,000 feet of educational war films during World War 2. The huge amount of cartoons was made possible by highly efficient methods of production (see Illus. 2 in appendix). [15] Also, the fairly cheap techniques, literally, helped the former "fantasy factory" turn into an industrial plant. [16]

Overall, Disney's reality-based films during wartime can be separated into two groups: Firstly, the instructional cartoons, produced for segments of the military, were light-hearted, yet having rather serious messages which aimed at soldiers, civilians, and defense workers. For example, they dealt with "recycling, hygiene, riveting techniques, or anti-tank weapons".[17]

In order to gain a proper knowledge for the training shorts, some staff members were even educated by officers and experts of the Navy and the Army (see Illus. 3 in appendix). Next to cartoon characters, those shorts also contained animated graphs and charts, and live characters. Apparently, they severely shortened the training period and enabled a "more comprehensive knowledge of technique". [18] After all, Disney's cartoon technique allowed its viewers to look inside something hard to be shown with cameras. [19]

Secondly, propagandist shorts, mostly brought about as "edutainment", rather talked to the broad mass of US-American citizens. From spring 1942 on, Disney educated the public with cartoons, such as *Food Will Win the War* or *Out of the Frying Pan into the Firing Line,* urging farmers to work for the war effort or housewives to save kitchen grease. More influential, however, were cartoons with a focus on entertainment that combined light-hearted and patriotic elements. Looking at the life in the armed forces (as in *Donald Gets Drafted* and *Commando Duck*), or satirically attacking the Axis

---

[14] Cf. Watts, The Magic Kindom: Walt Disney and the American Way of Life, p. 228
[15] Cf. Churchill, Walt Disney's Animated War, p. 50
[16] Cf. Watts, The Magic Kingdom: Walt Disney and the American Way of Life, p. 229
[17] Van Riper (Ed.), Learning from Mickey, Donald and Walt: Essays on Disney's Edutainment Films, p. 5
[18] Cf. Churchill, Walt Disney's Animated War, p. 50f, p. 136
[19] Cf. Anonymous, Walt Disney Goes to War, p. 61

powers (as in *Reason and Emotion* and *Der Fuehrer's Face*), those shorts "showcased the Disney Studio's contribution to the war effort and polished its image in the public eye".[20]

Apparently, the edutainment did not leave its audience unaffected. Having watched *The Spirit of '43,* an edutainment cartoon about decently saving money to be able to pay one's taxes to the US Government, for instance, a third of the viewership admitted to have followed the short's request. Reaching a broad part of the population was fairly easy as two-thirds went to the movies every week. Beginning in 1942, Disney also designed insignia for the troops. In the following years, Disney characters were widely regarded as "symbols of the American way of life, of freedom and of democracy" in the United States and allied nations. [21]

3.2. Walt Disney's propaganda ideas

Walt Disney's expectations towards educating and entertaining propaganda material were clear: it had to be "information-rich, yet lively and engaging". [22] Consequently, Life magazine called him a "visionary and practical artist", teaching the viewers, while cleverly holding their interest by the means of laughing and learning. He seemed to stubbornly follow the vision of a "world where a free popular art, using man's unlimited imagination, can flourish". [23]

Disney's apparent ideal was to create "democratic art", helping the militant conflict between democracy and dictatorships be won. Hence, while production, the principles of a free speech – so suggestions and criticism of the staff members- were dearly welcomed. However, Disney also recognized that the "medium he [was] still perfecting [was] greater than himself". Though he considered the possibilities to be limitless, he happily stepped onto new pathways. [24]

In general, Disney, as all of Hollywood, stood in for one central message, giving America courage: "Hang in there! We'll win if you all pitch in. This war is your war!"[25] By ridiculing the enemy and letting the audiences laugh at their own daily lives, his ideas and his effort were highly important to the people's morale.

---

[20] Watts, The Magic Kindom: Walt Disney and the American Way of Life, pp. 229f
[21] Stillich, Walt Disney and the Art of WW2 Propaganda- Donald Versus Hitler, pp. 1f
[22] Van Riper (Ed.), Learning from Mickey, Donald and Walt: Essays on Disney's Edutainment Films, p. 4
[23] Anonymous, Walt Disney Goes to War, p. 61
[24]Cf. ebd., p. 68
[25] Stillich, Walt Disney and the Art of WW2 Propaganda- Donald Versus Hitler, p. 2

4. Cartoon analysis

4.1. *Der Fuehrer's Face* (1943)

4.1.1 Content

Disney's propaganda short *"Der Fuehrer's Face"*[26], made in service of the US Government, was shown in theaters in 1943 and won an Oscar for the best animated short film in the same year.[27] The cartoon centers upon a nightmare of Donald Duck, encountering himself in "Nutziland" where he must work hard for Hitler's war effort.

On behalf of its content, the cartoon can be separated into three distinct parts: In part one, a Nazi marching band appears. Performing the "Der Fuehrer's Face"-song, the band, consisting of German, Japanese, and Italian musicians, glorifies Nutziland and Hitler, also proclaiming his new world order (see Illus. 4 in appendix).

Donald –still deeply asleep- is finally woken up by an alarm clock. A bayonet forces him out of bed, where he salutes to portraits of Hitler, Mussolini, and Hirohito. Trembling back to bed, a voice-over frightens him away with a bucket of cool water. After having dressed up unwillingly, Donald goes to have breakfast. Next to a single coffee bean, he solely finds "Aroma of Bacon and Eggs", and a dried-out piece of bread he can hardly chew (see Illus. 5 and 6 in appendix). While eating, the unknown voice hands in "Mein Kampf" as a lecture "to improve the mind" [3:02]. All the sudden, the marching band enters Donald's shack and makes him come along (with great aversion).

The second part begins in [3:23]: Fearfully, Donald is taken to a Nazi industrial plant, blowing clouds of steam into the red sky above. A voice-over reveals workers have to "work 48 hours a day for the Fuehrer" [3:30], while bayonets are pushing Donald towards an assembly line, supervised by a crowd of armed Nazis. From now on, shells in variable sizes and shapes pass Donald which he has to finish up. Whenever a Hitler portrait occurs on the assembly line, however, the ducks is compelled to do the Nazi salute (see Illus. 7 in appendix). Donald turns out to get more and more exhausted, when the voice-over promises a "vacation weekday" [5:28] in front of a poster of the Alps, being rolled out on the wall. In order "to work harder for the Fuehrer" [5:39], Donald even has to do physical activities "on vacation".

After being forced to work overtime, the rushed and stressed out Donald shouts: "I can't stand it! I can't stand it! I'm going mad! Stop! Stop! Stop! "[6:17]. At once, he drifts away into a chaotic, insane, and hectic dream world, dominated by shells, assembly

---

[26] Disney, Der Fuehrer's Face, www.youtube.com/watch?v=uXVDImhcy-4
[27] Cf. ebd., p. 1

lines, Hitler, and other Nazi symbolism. With a big bang, Donald bursts into smaller pieces and floats down to earth.

In the final part, starting [7:10], Donald wakes up in his, obviously, US-American room, realizing he has just had a nightmare of going to Nutziland. With relief he states: "Am I glad to be a citizen of the United States of America" [7:30] (see Illus. 8 in appendix). The cartoon ends with a tomato thrown at Hitler's face.

4.1.2. Shots, stylistic devices/figures, tone, and the effect on the viewer

As most of Disney's war-time cartoons, *"Der Fuehrer's Face"* represents an example of edutainment, both entertaining and educating its viewers.[28] Consequently, the tone is rather satirical and light-hearted because both the leaders of the Axis and the presumed lifestyle in "Nutziland" are exaggeratedly ridiculed.

Paying close attention while watching, Nazi symbolism, such as swastikas, helmets, Hitler's moustache etc., can be found in nearly every shot. Even the clouds and bushes have to adapt to Hitler's "new world order". In general, the entire setting stands for his ideology, limiting personal liberties to a minimum and oppressing the individual. The main protagonist Donald Duck must experience this to his cost: Daily life and work are monitored and restricted from above, a food shortage forces him to have "Aroma of Bacon and Eggs" for breakfast, the work on a shell assembly line wears him out, and even the promising "vacation weekday" – the only opportunity for Donald to catch a breath in Nutziland- turns out to be a boot camp.

After waking up from his nightmare, the closing scene –in clear contrast- portrays US-American symbolism in its purest form: Donald's pajamas and the curtains are in the colors of the Star-Spangled Banner, a patchwork above his bed says "Home Sweet Home", and he ultimately embraces a miniature Statue of Liberty in front of the window. Donald's relief after waking up at home also delivers potential for identification because it promotes ideas of patriotism. Assuming that the audience will follow his example, the cartoon capitalizes on the so-called bandwagon effect. Eventually- the viewer understands-, liberty rules over oppression, and healthy patriotism defeats insane nationalism. The cartoon's main message is further undermined by Donald's -to some extent pompous and solemn- words: "Am I glad to be a citizen of the United States of America" [7:30]. Moreover, the catchy "Der Fuehrer's Face"-song by Spike Jones and

---

[28] Cf. Van Riper (Ed.), Learning from Mickey, Donald and Walt: Essays on Disney's Edutainment Films, p. 5

His City Slickers certainly helps the cartoon get memorability and makes its main messages stay in the viewers' minds. Considering the cartoon's satirical aspect, the smashed
tomato in Hitler's face hammers home a viewpoint of America's enemies as figures of
fun nobody has to really be afraid of. As it stresses both American qualities and the enemies' flaws, *Der Fuehrer's Face* can be seen as – simultaneously- black and white
propaganda. In brief, although the cartoon does not request its war-time viewers to do a
concrete job, such as seen in *Out of the frying pan into the firing line*, it certainly does
affect the citizens' attitude towards war and their commitment to the war effort by both
pointing at the oppressive brutality of their enemies abroad and stressing the all-
American ideals, most of all liberty and individualism, the US Forces were fighting for.

4.1.3. Historical background, events, personalities, and figures
On behalf of the historical correctness of *Der Fuehrer's Face,* first of all, "Nutziland" is
to be examined. Certainly, the overall setting must not be understood as a reliable depic-
tion of Germany and its acquired territories at this point in time, but as an image of a
totalitarian state and its reprisals, which the US officials wished to convey to their viewers. There are no factual information given about Germany's war-time industry, but
rather logical assumptions are expressed.
Further, the leaders of the so-called Axis can be found and identified several times within the short: Whereas the Italian dictator Mussolini and the Japanese emperor Hirohito
only show up in the marching band and on the wall in Donald's shack, the clear focus is
on the German "Fuehrer" Adolf Hitler, who is the main personality to be mocked in the
short:
In the fall of 1940, Japan signed the Tri-Partite Agreement with Germany and Italy,
hereby, creating the Axis. However, "both the Japanese and the Germans grossly under-
estimated the United States and overestimated their own abilities in the face of the coali-
tion they had forced into existence", as further years of war would show. [29]
According to Hakim, the Axis powers' feeling of superiority came to light in the tactic
they approached their enemies: Like a wolf which picks up one sheep after the other
(not an entire flock at once), the Axis pursued one-by-on attacks on other nations, mostly democracies. While US-American military remained weak up until 1941, the "Berlin-
Rome-Tokyo Axis" could build up strong armies and air forces to attack their oppo-
nents. At once, in the end of 1941, the United States were caught in between a two-front

---

[29] Findling, Thackeray (Ed.), Events That Changed America, pp. 62, 69

war, looking west towards East Asia and the Pacific theater, and glancing East towards Western Europe and the European theater. Luckily however, from 1943 on, the year *Der Fuehrer's Face* was published, the Allies started finding ways to force back the apparently invincible Axis.[30]

4.2. *Reason and Emotion* (1943)

4.2.1. Content

Walt Disney's propaganda cartoon *"Reason and Emotion"*[31], as well as *Der Fuehrer's Face* produced for the US Government, was published in 1943.[32] The short deals with the two main counterparts of the human mind, Reason and Emotion, who are in permanent conflict with each other. In the Nazi's brain, however, Emotion has taken over, making its host be a thoughtless marionette of Hitler's instructions and demands.

In view of its content, the cartoon is split up into two parts: In part one, the main protagonists- Reason and Emotion- are introduced who "within the mind of each of us wage a ceaseless battle for mastery" [0:24]. In early childhood, Emotion, portrayed by a red-haired caveman, is having sole power in the child's mind, making it drop a flower vase from the window-sill, pull a cat's tail, or take a ride down the stairs. However, when Reason, a neatly dressed, sensible, and bespectacled scholar, appears, the battle begins. In adulthood, "Reason seems to be in the driver's seat with Emotion under control" [1:54] (see Illus. 9 in appendix). When the grown-up passes a pretty woman on the sidewalk, Emotion decides to steal back control. But the primitive come-on results in a slap by the addressed. Within her mind, female versions of Reason and Emotion vividly discuss the reaction on the male's advance. As seen before, Emotion, at once, obtains the driver's seat, conducting the woman towards food; hereby, she is led into obesity.

The second part starts [4:18]: An average American, John Dokes, is introduced who "tries to keep up with current events" [4:29], studying the newspaper, listening to the radio, and considering rumors and stories of his environment. While the highly contradictory information about the state of war confuse, overwhelm, and petrify Mr. Dokes on the outside, Reason and Emotion argue on the inside, too (see Illus. 10 in appendix). Before Emotion can gain the upper hand, the voice-over starts explaining the two of them how Hitler "destroys Reason by playing upon the weakness of Emotion with fear, sympathy, pride, and hate" [5:26]. In the mind of a Nazi, Hitler triggers fear of the con-

---

[30] Cf. Hakim, War, Peace, and All That Jazz, pp. 114, 126, 128, 134, 143, 158
[31] Disney, Reason and Emotion, http://www.youtube.com/watch?v=nad6dNA_0Ro
[32] Cf. Watts, The Magic Kingdom: Walt Disney and the American Way of Life, p. 230

centration camps and the Gestapo, evokes sympathy by pretending to be peace-loving, proclaims pride in "racial theories about Arian superiority" [6:22], and causes hate of the world's democracies (see Illus. 11-14 in appendix) . Thanks to the lecture, the American versions of Reason and Emotion seem to have understood. In the mind of an Air Force pilot, they are now able to co-operate, aiming for "the difficult course to victory" [7:30]. The final shot shows an immense Air Force fleet, flying along a bright sky (see Illus. 15 in appendix).

4.2.2. Shots, stylistic devices/figures, tone, and the effect on the viewer

Regarding the short's effect on the viewer, first of all, entertainment plays the most important role as no specific task to be done for the war is endorsed. Yet, the filmmakers apparently hope for a critical questioning of one's war-time emotions, such as the fear of defeat, and the confusion through rumors. Pleading for the victory of reason, the cartoon gives courage and confidence to the people. The air fleet in the end further symbolically embodies American strength and determination.

Accordingly, the tone in the first part is rather light-hearted and humorous; the audience is expected to relate itself with the daily struggles in the protagonists' minds, analyzed by literally climbing inside an infant's, a male's, and a female's head. In several close-ups, car-like equipped cross-sections of human heads– one of various ingenious visual ideas- give the setting for the funnily exaggerated personifications of everyone's psyche, Reason and Emotion. Clearly, Reason portrays the means of respect and restraint, being a strong contradiction to Emotion's anger and primitive desire. In the second part, which starts out with a cross-fade, however, the tone rather shifts towards seriousness as the ongoing war theater is brought up. Also, self-criticism and, finally, a patriotic, even solemn or pathetic atmosphere are evoked.

Intentionally, the tone is skilfully uttered by the background music, fitting in with the characters' moods. In infancy, for instance, the well-known sounds of *Twinkle, Twinkle Little Star* arouse. When Mr. Dotes shows up, in contrast, hectic and befuddled tunes predominate.

Overall, the cartoon is narrated by an omniscient, know-it-all voice-over narrator. He both addresses the viewers and the characters in a direct, frank manner; consequently, the narrator functions as a connecting link between storyline and auditorium. Whereas he explicitly informs the viewers about the processes in everybody's head, explains connections, and fills in the gaps, the main protagonists, Reason and Emotion, mostly experience a lecture about how an overly powerful emotion can cause terrible damage. In order to make his point, the narrator lists the feelings which Hitler plays upon in a Nazi's mind to gain power, simultaneously destroying Reason. Of course, while the characters in the cartoon have their epiphany, the viewer –implicitly addressed- understands to refer the described circumstances in Germany to his daily life: Even in times of war, common sense must not be taken over by our emotions. This message is further supported by the protagonists directly facing the camera in the meantime.

4.2.3. Historical background, events, personalities, and figures

Historically, the cartoon stresses the people's confusion when dealing with current events and rumors during the years from 1941 to 1945, so the timeframe of US-American participation in the war. In previous years, diplomatic relationships between America and Japan had been deteriorating. When Japan proposed a summit conference in 1941, the US agreed, yet demanding a Japanese withdrawal from China. Not at all willing to do so, Japanese officials began planning a first hostility which would –sooner than later- start the presumably inevitable war with the United States. [33]

The traumatizing event that forced America into the war was Pearl Harbor. On December 7, 1941, the Japanese Air Force launched a surprise attack on the American Pacific Fleet stationed at Pearl Harbor, Hawaii. During the assault, the Japanese managed to destroy almost all planes and warships, and caused thousands of casualties. Due to Pearl Harbor, isolationism – the widespread wish of US-American neutrality in the war- was soon replaced by internationalism- the cry for vengeance and involvement in the war in Asia and Europe. On December 8, 1941, President Roosevelt asked Congress for a declaration of war, calling Pearl Harbor an "unprovoked and dastardly attack". [34]

But, of course, the United States fiercely defied their enemies in the upcoming years. As, to some extent, portrayed in *Reason and Emotion*, the mobilization for a "modern industrial war"[35] and the inclusion of America's huge population gave evidence of the United States' total war effort. For these means, for instance, more than 275,000 airplanes were merchandized- some of them showed off in the closing sequence of the cartoon.

In spite of the permanent fear of physical attacks on the homeland and the dystopia of defeat, most Americans regarded World War 2 as their "good war". According to

---

[33] Cf. Findling, Thackeray (Ed.), Events That Changed America, pp. 62f
[34] Hakim, War, Peace, and All That Jazz, pp. 131-133
[35] Findling, Thackeray (Ed.), Events That Changed America, p.69

Thornton, "the war was fought far from their towns, shores, and homes, which allowed Americans to view their fight as one for values like freedom and justice while the Soviets and others fought for survival".[36] Among those were people who did not fit in with Hitler's idea of Arian supremacy. Regarding Germans and other "Arian" peoples as the "master race", Hitler -as well-portrayed in the short- claimed the right to conquer "living space" in the East and enslave others.[37] In concentration camps, political enemies (caught up by Hitler's secret police, the Gestapo) and, later on, minorities, such as Jews or gypsies, were cruelly tortured and executed. The true extent of atrocities, however, did not reveal itself to the Allies until the post-war period.

6. Was it justified to "misuse" family cartoons as propaganda material?

When thinking about the huge impact US-American propaganda –especially Disney's shorts- had on the citizens, one might wonder whether it was overall justified to make use of the cartoons as propaganda material. After all, Disney's cartoons had solely been family entertainment in the pre-war period. The pros and cons of this question will now be discussed.

On the one hand, some badly-informed or uneducated viewers might not have recognized the shorts as propaganda, adopting Mickey's or Donald's viewpoints without critically questioning them. Employing well-known and beloved figures to convey messages for the US Government, Disney capitalized on the so-called bandwagon effect which made particular citizens think and act like the characters.

In addition, the overly light-hearted cartoons, to some extent, overshadowed the true hazards radiating from Europe and Asia. Hereby, they created an unrealistic feeling of invincibility, instead of admitting vulnerability.

On the other hand, however, the combination of funny entertainment and serious messages – also known as "edutainment" – helped the morals and instructions stick in mind more easily. For instance, Donald's call for patriotism in *Der Fuehrer's Face* would have been less effective without satirically ridiculing Hitler and "Nutziland".

Moreover, well-known figures from other Disney productions –oftentimes- served as role models within the shorts to which the viewers could perfectly relate. Consequently, it was easier to identify with the characters and their ideas for the war effort.

---

[36] Cf. ebd., pp. 73f
[37] Cf. Hakim, War, Peace, and All That Jazz, p. 136

The fact that cartoons were fairly cheap and easier to produce than real-life shorts further undermines their right to exist. Whereas real-life movies demanded a costly staff, props, and scenery, cartoons could be easily drawn on paper.

Also, cartoon shorts reached a broad audience in the United States. Besides being loved by all generations, it was highly effective to play them before major movies as many Americans (close to 100 million viewers, nearly two-thirds of the population) went to the movies on a weekly basis by then.

Yet most importantly, Disney's propaganda shorts did support and spread a way of thinking still valid today. Democracy, liberty, and the denial of totalitarian systems and absurd ideologies are considered as essential principles in most Western societies. By delivering those messages, Disney's war-time cartoons, obviously, helped the good ones win the war.

In conclusion, I must exert my firm agreement with Disney's presumed family cartoons to be used as propaganda material. Although they were persuasively constructed–not factually or argumentatively- and skillfully made their viewers adopt the messages, they were certainly created for a good purpose, namely defeating the megalomaniacal Axis powers. Especially the philosophy of "edutainment" and the general popularity of Disney characters fostered Uncle Sam's appeal to work hard for victory.

7. Recapping the results

Coming to the end of my 'Facharbeit', I would like to recap the obtained knowledge and draw overall conclusions: In the days of World War 2, propagandists seated in nearly every department of the US Government intended to spread two main messages, mostly using mass media: the fight between dictatorship and democracy and the possible fruits of victory. The Disney Studios greatly contributed to that distribution by making a total of 400,000 feet of film for the government. Mainly, Disney's philosophy was to create "democratic art", defending the supremacy of democracy and being produced democratically. Whereas some cartoons were of instructional nature, others had rather propagandist aims, melting light-hearted and seriously patriotic elements into the genre of edutainment.

Both *Der Fuehrer's Face* and *Reason and Emotion* exemplify the entertaining niche of Disney's war-time cartoons, while also having a solemn and patriotic ending. Mixing black and white propaganda, they do not fear ridiculing the Axis and wholeheartedly promote America's strength. In doing so, they employ many visual exaggerations and a lot of symbolism. Regarding the cartoons' differences, *Reason and Emotion* -once in a while- expresses a self-critical tone, whereas *Der Fuehrer's Face* is only critical of totalitarian systems, Nazi Germany in particular. Here, it is seen as a gloomy, nightmarish place called "Nutziland", while *Reason and Emotion* uses Germany as a stage to lecture the viewer about the necessity to get ahold of one's emotions. Moreover, in *Der Fuehrer's Face*, the protagonist's war-time struggles and hardships are presented right in the beginning, which does not happen until the second half of *Reason and Emotion*.

Not unnaturally, these two shorts were highly respected and appreciated by the public, even - as in the case of *Der Fuehrer's Face*- winning an Academy Award. As 100 million citizens went to the movies on a weekly basis, Disney's propaganda shorts were able to reach the broad masses. Consequently, their overall effect on the citizens' morale must be called immense (with a few exceptions like my Kansan host grandmother): The shorts motivated and encouraged the population to personally contribute to the war effort, giving the comforting confidence that the war would end in victory. Clearly, they were created for a good purpose as they wanted to help defeat the Axis powers by - mostly- using well-known Disney characters. With regard to the analyzed cartoons, both examples pick the audiences up from a state of fear and confusion, guiding them towards a brighter vision of the future.

8. Bibliography

Primary Sources:

DISNEY, Walt, Der Fuehrer's Face, 1943, uploaded on: 09/03/2008, retrieved on: 01/20/2014, URL: www.youtube.com/watch?v=uXVDImhcy-4

DISNEY, Walt, Reason and Emotion, 1943, uploaded on: 09/06/2012, retrieved on: 02/23/2014, URL: http://www.youtube.com/watch?v=nad6dNA_0Ro

REIMER, Gladys, personal correspondence, received on: 01/19/2014

Secondary Sources:

ANONYMOUS, Walt Disney Goes to War, in: Life magazine 1942 (No. 9), pp. 61 – 69

BREWER, Susan A., Why America fights: patriotism and war propaganda from the Philippines to Iraq, New York (Oxford University Press) 2009

CHURCHILL, Edward, Walt Disney's Animated War, in: Flying 1945 (No. 3), pp. 50f, 134, 136, 138

FINDLING, John E., THACKERAY, Frank W. (Ed.), Events that changed America in the twentieth century, Westport (Greenwood Press) 1996, 3. Edition

HAKIM, Joy, War, Peace, and All That Jazz (1918-1945), New York (Oxford University Press) 2003, 3. Edition

KRANZ, PALAND, TEPE (Ed.), Password to Skyline Plus- Lesebuch zur Einführung in die Oberstufenarbeit, Stuttgart (Klett) 2001

KUHN, Annette, WESTWELL, Guy, A Dictionary of Film Studies, Oxford (Oxford University Press) 2012

MCLEAN, Iain, MCMILLAN, Alistair, The Concise Oxford Dictionary of Politics, Oxford (Oxford University Press) 2009, 3. Edition

VAN RIPER, A. Bowdoin (Ed.), Learning from Mickey, Donald and Walt: Essays on Disney's Edutainment Films, Jefferson (McFarland) 2011

WATTS, Steven, The Magic Kingdom: Walt Disney and the American Way of Life, Columbia (University of Missouri Press) 2001

WRIGHT, Edmund (Ed.), A Dictionary of World History, Oxford (Oxford University Press) 2006, 2. Edition

STILLICH, Sven, Walt Disney and the Art of WW2 Propaganda- Donald Versus Hitler, uploaded on: 08/10/2009, retrieved on: 01/28/2014, URL: http://www.spiegel.de/international/germany/donald-versus-hitler-walt-disney-and-the-art-of-wwii-propaganda-a-641547.html